D0402935

THE Fourth GIFT

A Christmas Story

THE Fourth GIFT

A Christmas Story

J. TUCKER DAVIS

Bonneville Books
Springville, Utah

ISBN 13: 978-1-59955-438-9

Published by Bonneville Books, an imprint of Cedar Fort, Inc., 2373 W. 700 S., Springville, UT 84663
Distributed by Cedar Fort, Inc., www.cedarfort.com
LIBRARY OF CONGRESS CATALOGING-IN-PUBLICATION DATA
Davis, J. Tucker, 1947-
The fourth gift : a Christmas story / J. Tucker Davis.
p. cm.
Summary: An orphaned shepherd boy gives a prized possession to the Christ Child.
ISBN 978-1-59955-438-9 (acid-free paper)
[1. Shepherds--Fiction. 2. Orphans--Fiction. 3. Jesus Christ--Nativity--Fiction.] I. Title.

PZ7.D28847Fo 2010
[Fic]--dc22
                2010015433

Cover design by Megan Whittier
Cover painting "Silent Night" by Joseph Brickey (2000)
Cover design © 2010 by Lyle Mortimer
Edited and typeset by Heidi Doxey

Printed in the United States of America

10 9 8 7 6 5 4 3 2 1

Printed on acid-free paper

Dedicated as a Christmas gift
to my beloved family.

✳

He was called the Christ, the long-awaited Messiah.
His birth marked the meridian of time.
Heir to the throne of David, He came to save a world.
In the Greek, His name was Jesus.
But to His people and His family,
He was simply known by a common Aramaic name.
His advent was God's gift to us.

✳

This is the story of a young boy who shared in that
momentous first Christmas.

Chapter One

There was no moon, but the stars spilled across the sky like Solomon's jewels. By their light, young Jeshua Barnabas nimbly picked his way up the hillside. He paused and turned to look down on the little city that was his home. Its windows shone with the light of countless lamps; the ruddy glow of torches and cooking fires burnished its walls and streets. The sweet smell of evening meals cooking on the hearths teased Jeshua's nose. He glanced eagerly at the pot he carried for Eleazar, the old shepherd. He would not go hungry tonight.

The city had filled to overflowing with visitors responding to the decree of some great emperor far away. Camps and tents blossomed on the city's outskirts. With night, the cacophony of the day had stilled to an exotic murmur of foreign voices, strange music, and the braying and lowing of unfamiliar animals.

The day's begging had been good. Jeshua rattled the coins in the leather pouch he wore about his neck, tucked safely beneath his tunic. Nestled in that pouch were all of his worldly treasures—his few coins mingled with the small assorted odds and ends collected by an orphan boy. Most of the items, though of nearly incalculable worth in Jeshua's mind, were the mere refuse of others. His most precious possession, however, was a rather expertly carved little wooden lamb, fashioned by Jeshua's father as a toy for his young son. Jeshua sometimes took the lamb out of his pouch to admire it, although he never could quite bring himself to play with it as he had when he was much younger. He kept it wrapped in a bit of cloth to protect it from being nicked by any of the other items in the pouch.

Jeshua breathed deeply of the evening air. The spring nights had become mild, heralding the birth of the firstlings of the flocks. And so Eleazar and the other shepherds were in the fields, keeping special watch over the ewes and their lambs. Eleazar's wife, Naomi, often asked Jeshua to carry the old man's meal to him, and she always took care to put in extra for the orphan boy as well.

Jeshua looked up at the star-laden heavens. A little shiver slipped down his spine. He did not know why, but the night seemed pregnant with promise beyond that of merely a warm meal.

Again he scampered up the hillside. His nine-year-old legs were tireless. He quickly reached the crest, ran across a little vale, and began ascending a larger hill that rose behind the first. Now he could hear the bleating of the sheep. Halfway up the second hill, he stopped short, startled—his shadow had abruptly appeared before him! Where a moment before he had barely been able to discern the trail in the darkness, now his path was ablaze in light. A little frightened, he gazed warily around. The whole landscape glistened, bathed in an ethereal whiteness. He timidly glanced over his shoulder. There, in the heavens, appeared the cause of this sudden light—a radiant new star had been born. It shone more brightly than all of the others, its lustrous rays cascading over the earth. Awestruck, Jeshua stumbled and fell backward, but his eyes remained riveted on this fulgent wonder.

In all of his young life, Jeshua had never beheld such a magnificent sight. Minutes passed as he contemplated the star. What could it possibly mean? He had heard that signs in the heavens often portend great events on earth. This new star shimmered with such ferocity that surely some monumental thing must be about to transpire. But what?

So transfixed was he by the star that, for a time, Jeshua was scarcely aware of the singing that now echoed down from the hills. The anthem flowed rich and sonorous, plucking at the very chords of his heart. He craned his head toward the fields where the flocks were kept. Surely this was not the shepherds singing; mere mortals were not capable of music such as this. Jeshua trembled. He was astonished as his eyes filled with warm tears. He could not quite hear the words, but the music, more exalted than any he had ever heard, quickened his soul.

Rarely had he been to synagogue, but the night suddenly seemed so holy that Jeshua pulled his frayed shawl over his head and quickly uttered a prayer. He knew not whence came the music, nor why this new star shone, but he felt something ignite within him. Something sublime, elevating. This night was surely like no other.

The singing ceased. Who could have produced such glorious strains? His pulse quickened. What lay behind the hill? Excitement welled within him, but he continued to feel a little frightened. Mustering his courage, he tentatively resumed his way up the hill. The star illuminated his path almost like day. He trod slowly, as if the ground itself were sacred.

The shepherds' camp was in commotion when Jeshua arrived. Eleazar, for all of his years, was ebullient. He beckoned to Jeshua. "Jeshua, did you see them? We have just been visited by a heavenly host! Jeshua, the day of our deliverance is at hand—the Messiah is born! What great tidings! Oh, that I have lived to see this day!"

Eleazar gasped for breath and placed a trembling hand on Jeshua's shoulder. "My boy, did you hear the angel speak?"

"I . . . I heard singing."

"Oh, yes, Jeshua. The angels themselves were singing!" Eleazar looked upward. " *'Glory to God in the highest, and on earth peace, good will toward men!'* Those were the words they spoke to us. They spoke to *us*, mere shepherds! Our king, our Savior, is come! What a blessed night! Come, Jeshua, we leave now to worship the child. The angel said we should find Him this night in a manger, in our own beloved City of David."

The other shepherds bustled around the camp, extinguishing cooking fires, storing belongings in their tents, and arraying themselves in their best robes. Some looked for gifts to bring. Jeshua stowed Naomi's pot by Eleazar's tent.

Eleazar hurried to one of his lambing pens. "Jeshua, help me! We must take the firstling of my flock as an offering for our newborn king!" He pointed to one of the lambs.

Jeshua obediently climbed into the stone pen. The ewe protested, but he soon had the little lamb in his arms. The lamb bleated but quieted as Jeshua petted him.

Jeshua and Eleazar joined the other shepherds as they made their way down from the fields. Jeshua was breathless with exhilaration. He did not quite grasp it all, but the Deliverer, the Savior, whom he knew everyone had been awaiting for a very long time, had apparently been born at last. And Jeshua, the beggar boy, was going with the shepherds to see that young personage, who evidently was also a king. "The King of Kings!" observed Eleazar as he leaned on the boy to make his way down the starlit path. "The King of Kings!"

Chapter Two

*J*eshua had long regarded certain homes in Bethlehem as palatial. Not being entirely sure about what a
manger was but possessing definite ideas as to where kings
would normally be accommodated, he naturally supposed
that the shepherds were journeying to one of those great
houses. He therefore found himself somewhat confused
when his party began searching the area where much of the
town's livestock was quartered.

When at last the shepherds located the place, the lowly
surroundings distressed Jeshua. It was nothing more than
a humble stable, recessed into the hillside. The door was
ajar, and a couple of windows were partially covered by
hides that had been tacked over them. The stable was
old, ramshackle, and smelled no different than others of
its kind. The window coverings did not conceal the odor
that had accumulated over many years of housing countless animals.

"But, Eleazar," Jeshua said, "this is a stable! This is no place for a king!"

"Ah, my boy, did not the prophet Zechariah teach that the king would be 'lowly,' as well as 'just, and having salvation'? Is it not also written that 'before honour is humility'? The angel told us that we should find the babe 'lying in a manger.' Look, my boy, yonder He lies, wrapped in swaddling clothes!"

And, indeed, through the open door Jeshua saw the newborn babe, nestled in the hay of a trough. The shepherds respectfully approached the entrance to the stable. As Jeshua drew closer, he thought to himself that at least the hay smelled sweet. But then he thought about it being the same hay used to feed the animals. He continued to have qualms about the adequacy of a stable for this royal birth.

As the shepherds crowded into the doorway, Jeshua worried that they might be intruding. The infant, after all, had clearly just been born. The mother was to one side, with her head bowed. A shepherd stepped in front of Jeshua, blocking, for the moment, Jeshua's view of the man standing behind and to the right of the woman.

As Jeshua surveyed the rest of the lowly stable, it did not look at all suitable for the Savior of the world. Abruptly, however, he again experienced those feelings of holiness he had felt earlier in the evening. This was truly only a stable, but there was a peace, and even a majesty, to the scene before him. He glanced at the several animals in the stable. Even they seemed to pay reverence to Him who had been born.

The lamp now caught the face of the young woman. She

was the most beautiful woman Jeshua had ever beheld. He could not remember his own mother, but the sweet face he always saw in his dreams bore the same loving countenance of this woman. She beamed at her newborn. Jeshua scrutinized her lovely features. Her face radiated the adoration and love that Jeshua had often longed to receive from his own departed mother. A little lump crept into his throat.

He peered further around the shepherd in front of him. The man in the stable, whose humble dress could not conceal a quiet dignity, lightly rested his sinewy hand on the shoulder of the young woman in front of him. His gentle eyes regarded the infant and His mother with warmth and a boundless joy. Those eyes looked familiar to Jeshua. He had seen them somewhere before. But where?

Then he remembered. Earlier, while he had been begging in the streets, Eleazar had asked him to help move some of the sheep from the pasture to the pens. As Jeshua had herded the little flock through the hills, he had seen this couple near the road that led to Bethlehem. The man had looked at him and nodded. The woman, who had been riding a donkey, had looked at Jeshua too, but much of her face had been covered against the dust of the road. They surely had been making their way to the city.

Jeshua looked for Eleazar. He wanted to whisper to the old shepherd about his prior encounter with the babe's parents. But the lamb Jeshua carried had decided at that moment that there was too much of a crowd in the doorway and nearly wriggled free.

The woman looked up and briefly caught Jeshua's eye.

He shyly ducked behind the shepherd who stood in front of him. She looked at the rest of the shepherds and gently smiled. She beckoned them to come closer.

The man in the stable also smiled and welcomed the shepherds. "Peace be unto you. I am Joseph Bar-Heli, of Nazareth. And this is my wife, Maryam."

Eleazar, who was the oldest of the shepherds, had by now entered the stable. He made a low bow. "And peace be unto you, as well. We are but humble shepherds and are come to see Him who is born our Messiah."

Maryam's eyes met Joseph's. The barest whisper of apprehension flickered across their faces. Angelic proclamations had advised them both of the child's divine mission, but they had not expected others to know so quickly. It took no leap of imagination to realize that Herod's kingdom might be a very dangerous place for the rightful heir to the throne of David. Knowledge of the child's birth could put Him in dire jeopardy. Yet, here were shepherds who already knew.

Eleazar studied them both, saw the look that passed between them. "An angel brought us these 'good tidings of great joy.' And said that unto us is born 'a Saviour, which is Christ the Lord.' "

Maryam and Joseph appeared to relax. God had sent these shepherds.

Joseph bade them gather close to the manger. "This," he gestured reverently, "is the newborn child."

The shepherds crept forward and fell to their knees. Those who had brought lambs now offered them to the holy family. Some whispered, "Hosanna!" Some uttered, "Blessed be the King of Israel!" And some echoed, "Hosanna in the highest!"

Eleazar turned and beckoned for Jeshua to come forward with the lamb. Jeshua timidly complied and handed the little lamb to Eleazar, who stooped and placed the animal before the child. "Blessed is He that cometh in the name of the Lord!" he said.

A look of wonder, tinged with some concern, crossed Maryam's face as she pondered the adoration of the shepherds. Her eyes moistened slightly. The presence of the shepherds somehow made the child's mission more imminent. Still, she was grateful that others were here on this holy night, that the child had not been born in complete ignominy. She reached into the manger and held the child up for His visitors.

Jeshua's timidity was quickly overcome by his curiosity, and he deftly slipped to the front of the group. From there he inspected the infant closely. The Deliverer bore no regal trappings—there were no jewels, not even a crown. Up close, He did not look fearsome or even majestic. He was but a cute little infant, wrapped in swaddling clothes.

"Has He a name yet?" Jeshua inquired, with the return of a boldness born of a life spent begging. Maryam looked at him, and recognition filled her eyes.

"Joseph," she said, "it is the boy we saw near the road."

Joseph nodded. Jeshua's face colored.

Maryam smiled at Jeshua. "A name has been chosen for Him. At his naming, He shall be called Jeshua."

"Jeshua?" The beggar boy caught his breath. "His name will be the same as mine!" he shouted to his shepherd friend, who motioned in vain for him to lower his voice. "Eleazar, He has the same name as I!" Jeshua, who had no kin, beamed at the child as if He were a little brother.

Maryam looked again at Jeshua. She appeared gratified by the young boy's exuberance. The babe, still cradled in Maryam's arms, likewise seemed to regard the beggar boy.

"My son," said Maryam, "since you and He shall share the same name, perhaps you may one day be friends." She knew, perhaps better than anyone, that her young child would have need of friends in His lifetime.

Jeshua was thrilled. "Oh, I will be a friend to Him!"

"I'm afraid He's too little now for you to play with," Maryam said. "But when He's older, perchance there may be opportunity for the two of you to play together. You'll be older too. It may be that He will need someone to watch over Him, to keep Him from any harm."

The shepherds looked at Jeshua with new interest. Young Jeshua, it appeared, had found favor with the Deliverer's mother. Eleazar smiled his approval. Jeshua was overwhelmed and ready to burst with pride.

"I would give my life to protect Him," he said soberly.

Eleazar reached over and placed his hand on Jeshua's shoulder. "Come, my boy, the child and His mother must rest now." He signaled the withdrawal of the shepherds and, gesturing to the family, he nodded. "Peace be unto you."

"And unto you," replied Joseph. He bowed his head and gestured toward the offerings left by the shepherds. "And thanks be unto you for the gracious gifts you have bestowed upon the child."

As the shepherds retreated, Jeshua repeatedly looked back at the Christ child, now resting again in the manger. Then he grinned at Eleazar. "He has the same name as I, Eleazar!"

Eleazar tousled the boy's hair. "Jeshua, remember this night well. You will tell your children's children about what transpired this holy night."

Chapter Three

S ome of the shepherds were eager to return to their flocks. Others, like Eleazar, sought first to relate to their families what had happened.

"Come, Jeshua, we must go tell my wife! We must tell Naomi what the new star signifies! She will be so surprised!"

Good Naomi was indeed surprised and even overwhelmed at the news, but not so much that she neglected to mention her distress over the fact that Eleazar and Jeshua had not yet found time to eat the supper she had labored much of the day to provide for them. She clucked disapprovingly.

"You both shall be ill with your bellies so empty, and so the flocks will be without a shepherd, and then what is to become of us, Deliverer or no? The Lord God Himself has declared that 'thou shall eat the labour of thine hands,' and what if you become too weak to labor, my dear Eleazar? I ask again, what then must become of us?"

"But, my dear, surely this should be a night of fasting!"

"Fasting! And after I arose at dawn to grind the meal . . . ." She paused and sputtered. "Would I have done that if this was to be a fast day, my dear husband? And would not the young Deliverer prefer us to *feast* on His coming? This surely should be a night of rejoicing, not one of deprivation!"

Naomi, regardless of the night's momentous tidings, was fiercely protective of her beloved husband, and so nothing would do but that she set a meal before him and Jeshua prior to their return to the fields. Eleazar found that he was too filled with the night's events to eat much, despite Naomi's protestations, but little Jeshua was famished, a fact which, notwithstanding her concern over Eleazar, appeared to please Naomi to no end.

"At least Jeshua seems to like my cooking!" she observed to Eleazar.

Jeshua took a piece of bread and wiped the very last of his food from the bowl. "My mistress, there is none who can cook as you!"

Naomi looked askance at Eleazar. "Why, Jeshua, I suspect that your words are borne of your hunger, but thank you, my dear."

Eleazar, perhaps trying to steer the conversation in a different direction, turned to Jeshua and asked, "So, Jeshua, you had already met the child's parents?"

"We passed near the road when I was taking the flock to pasture. The man nodded at me." Jeshua smiled. "I did not think they would remember me."

"Well, they certainly did seem to remember you. And they were kind to all of us. Imagine, Jeshua, we are but lowly shepherds and yet we were chosen to be given the tidings of the Savior's birth." Eleazar shook his head.

Despite Jeshua's full belly, he wanted to remain with the shepherds this night and thus prepared to accompany Eleazar back into the fields. As the two were about to depart, Naomi bustled in from the hearth.

"Jeshua, the Deliverer's family has traveled far, and the sweet mother has given birth in that filthy stable—I want you to take this pot of food to them before you return to the fields."

Jeshua looked at Eleazar. "It is night. Will you be able to make the climb into the hills without me?"

"My boy," Eleazar replied, "I have been making that climb since before I was your age. Naomi's idea is a good one. The Messiah's family cannot have had much to eat. You go to the stable and then join us in the fields."

Eleazar looked at Naomi. "My good wife, the children of Israel would not have needed manna had you been along. This is most thoughtful. You are a jewel among women."

Naomi blushed as she fussed at both of them. "Now, be off with you, Jeshua! Tell the new king's family where I live and that I will be home should they need anything. And you, Eleazar, mind that the dinner Jeshua brought you tonight does not go to waste!"

And so Eleazar returned to the fields, and young Jeshua Barnabas found his way back to a stable on the outskirts of Bethlehem. The stable's door had been closed, and less light shone through the partially covered windows. Jeshua peered through a corner of one window. He saw that the lamp hanging from a rafter had been trimmed. Maryam sat in the straw behind the manger with the babe cuddled in her arms. Joseph was feeding the donkey that had carried his wife from Nazareth.

Jeshua hoped that it was not too late to intrude. He meekly rapped on the stable door.

Joseph opened the door. "Peace be unto you," said Jeshua softly, bowing his head.

"And unto you," said Joseph. "Who is there?" he asked, peering into the darkness.

"Master, it is I, . . . Jeshua."

"Jeshua? The shepherd boy? Pray come in, my son."

Jeshua stepped inside the door. "Naomi, the wife of the good shepherd, Eleazar, bade me bring you this meal."

Joseph accepted the pot from the boy. He lifted the lid slightly and peeked inside.

"It smells wonderful, Jeshua. My wife is weak from the journey and the birth. This will do her much good." He turned. "Maryam, see what young Jeshua has brought us from the house of Eleazar and Naomi!"

Maryam appeared tired, but she smiled when she saw Jeshua. "Jeshua! Peace be unto you, my child."

"And unto you, my mistress."

"Welcome. And what is this that you have brought?"

"Naomi, the wife of the noble Eleazar, thought you might be hungry and had me bring you this meal."

"How very kind of her! We have only had bread to eat

today. Will you stay and share this supper with us?"

"Thank you, I have eaten, my mistress," said Jeshua. "And I must join Eleazar and the others in the fields. Naomi said that she will be home should you need anything. They live seven doors to the south of the inn."

The babe awakened and turned His head in the direction of Jeshua. Maryam shifted in the straw and pulled His homespun blanket more tightly around Him. The night had grown chilly.

Maryam looked again at Jeshua. "Please thank goodly Eleazar and Naomi for their kindness." She paused. "Are they your parents?"

"No, my mistress." Jeshua hesitated. "My . . . my parents are dead."

"Oh, Jeshua, I am sorry! Are they then your grandparents?"

"No, my mistress. They are not kin." He smiled slightly. "They are my friends."

"My dear, who then cares for you? Do you live with them?"

"No, my mistress." Jeshua lowered his eyes, and his face flushed. "I . . . I am but a beggar."

"Oh, Jeshua!" Maryam looked at Joseph and then again at Jeshua.

Joseph moved closer to Jeshua. "It is surely no dishonor to be a beggar, my son," he said. "This is no fault of yours." He put his arm about the boy. "Did not Isaiah declare, 'The poor among men shall rejoice in the Holy One of Israel'? I do not quite understand it myself, Jeshua, but this child," he looked at the infant with genuine wonder, "is a gift from our Father above unto us all. Jeshua, we are poor as well. This child comes to offer everyone the riches of heaven."

Jeshua looked again at the child. He felt the comforting warmth of Joseph's arm on his shoulder. A tear coursed down the side of his nose. He rarely cried, but for the second time this night, his eyes filled with tears. The holy family was kind. Aside from Eleazar and Naomi, he had not experienced much kindness during his young life.

Maryam said, "Jeshua, my son is come to unite us all in the family of God, our Father. His family shall be your family." She smiled.

Jeshua also smiled. He wiped his eyes with the back of his hand.

Maryam spoke again. "Here, would you like to hold your namesake?"

Jeshua was unsure. He had never even touched a baby. He wasn't certain how to handle one.

"Be not afraid, Jeshua," Maryam added sweetly. "Hold Him like this." She placed the infant in the boy's arms.

At first, Jeshua was scared. He didn't want to drop this child for whom the whole world had been waiting. But Maryam and Joseph reassured him.

The swaddled infant felt warm as He nestled against Jeshua's chest. "How small He is! His fingers are so tiny!" The beggar boy grinned. "Greetings, little Jeshua! I am Jeshua too."

The babe looked into Jeshua's face and cooed. "I think He likes me!" Jeshua beamed.

"I think so too," replied Maryam.

The boy gently rocked little Jeshua in his arms. "It will be hard for Him to be the Messiah, won't it?"

"I am afraid it may be, my son." A hint of sadness tinged Maryam's voice. "But God, His Father, will watch over Him." She smiled at Jeshua. "And He will have friends like you, Jeshua."

"I *will* be His friend," responded Jeshua. "I will look out for Him."

Jeshua leaned over and kissed the baby's forehead. "Thank you for letting me hold Him," said Jeshua. "I have never held a king before."

Maryam and Joseph smiled.

After Jeshua had bidden farewell to the family, he ran through the outskirts of Bethlehem. He fairly skipped up the path into the hills. His spirit was so buoyant that he feared he might fly right into the starlit sky should he take too long a stride.

The shepherds, and particularly Eleazar, listened intently to Jeshua's account of his second visit to the stable. They all agreed that Jeshua had been accorded a singular honor when he had been allowed to hold the Savior of the world.

Sleep did not come easily. The star was so bright, and the night's events had been momentous. The shepherds, clustered in little groups, continued to review what had transpired and what the birth of this child would mean for the empire, the kingdom, their own land of Judaea, and that old tyrant, King Herod.

Chapter Four

When Jeshua awoke the next morning, the sun had already chased the shadows from the hills, and the dew had fled on a warm spring breeze. The previous night seemed but a wonderful dream. Jeshua languidly stretched his arms.

Suddenly Jeshua's eyes snapped open. The events of the prior night poured back into his mind. It had not been a dream! He remembered all that had happened—vividly, intensely. He had *been* there! He had seen and even held the newborn king. Indeed, the king shared his own name.

He looked for Eleazar. The aged shepherd stood to the side of a nearby sycamine tree. His head and shoulders draped in his tallit, his hands outstretched, Eleazar rocked back and forth in prayer. No doubt he was praying about the birth of the Messiah. *Yes*, thought Jeshua, *it had surely been a night to remember.*

The other shepherds were tending the cooking fires, preparing to break the fast. Jeshua had eaten so well the night before that he didn't even feel hungry this morning.

Eleazar concluded his prayers and noticed Jeshua stirring.

"Jeshua, my boy," called Eleazar, "I thought you were going to sleep until tomorrow! I thought that perhaps the sun had again stood still upon Gibeon and you might never awaken!"

Jeshua flashed a diffident grin.

"Indeed," Eleazar continued, "as I recall, it was the prophet Joshua, your namesake in the Hebrew tongue of our fathers, who commanded that sun to stand still. I am sure *he* would be proud of a boy who sleeps the day away!"

"I am sure even the old prophet had to sleep sometimes," retorted Jeshua. He gave Eleazar a wink. "Besides, I can't be too bad of a boy since I share the old prophet's name with the Messiah himself!"

Eleazar chuckled. "No, my young Jeshua, I don't suppose you can. The child's mother certainly took a liking to you."

"Do you think she did?'

"Oh, I am certain of it. You told us last night that she even let you hold the babe. She didn't let any of us hold Him, now did she?"

Jeshua smiled. He helped Eleazar stoke the cooking fire. For breakfast they would eat the last of Naomi's meal from the night before.

"How soon do you think the young king will be crowned?" asked Jeshua.

"I don't know, Jeshua. I am but a simple shepherd. I do

not know about such things." Eleazar studied his hands. "However, I do worry about what that usurper, Herod, may do when he hears that one has been born King of the Jews. We've all told our families and others about the marvelous things that happened last night. Word may travel beyond Bethlehem." Eleazar hesitated. "Perhaps we should have been more careful—I don't know."

They ate in silence. Jeshua hoped that Herod would cause no problems for the little child and His noble family.

Jeshua passed the day helping with the flocks. He liked being in the hills—it was a relief from days spent begging. He coaxed reluctant ewes from their hiding places and into the pens where he helped Eleazar with the lambing. He directed the suckling of those little lambs who couldn't quite figure out where to secure their first meal. And he provided extra barley to the ewes so that their milk would be rich for their newborns.

At midday, Eleazar and Jeshua shared a loaf of bread and some cheese.

"I was thinking this morning, Jeshua, how very lucky we are to be witnesses to the birth of our little king," said Eleazar. "Our people have been awaiting His coming for a long time."

"How long, Eleazar?" asked Jeshua.

"Oh, a very long time, Jeshua. Since the Torah was first written by Moses."

"How long has that been?"

"It has been almost fifteen centuries since we came out of Egypt and were given the law. But many of the prophets have written of the Messiah since. The words of Isaiah came to me last night as I tried to sleep."

"The child's father spoke to me last evening of Isaiah. Was he a prophet?"

"Yes, and a very important one. He prophesied over seven hundred years ago."

"What did he say?"

"A great many things. But the words I thought of last night were about the child. It is a passage my father taught me."

"Can you recite it to me?" asked Jeshua.

"I still remember the verse. The prophet said, 'For unto us a child is born, unto us a son is given: and the government shall be upon his shoulder: and his name shall be called Wonderful, Counsellor, The mighty God, The everlasting Father, The Prince of Peace.' " Eleazar rubbed his brow. "Oh, would that He might bring us peace, Jeshua."

"Has King Herod read these words, Eleazar?"

"I do not know, Jeshua. I suspect he knows of them."

"Then he must know that the child is to be the rightful king."

"I am afraid that Herod will think more of his throne than the words, Jeshua."

"Perhaps we should warn the babe's parents, Eleazar."

"I have no doubt, Jeshua, that His parents know well the danger that King Herod may present."

Jeshua thoughtfully chewed on a morsel of bread. "Maybe God will send the angels back to protect the child."

"He may, Jeshua. God is all powerful."

"What did they look like, Eleazar—the angels you saw last night?"

"Well, at first there was only one. He was very bright. It was almost hard to look upon him, he shone so much. He was dressed in a white robe—all of the angels were. And his voice, Jeshua . . . his voice penetrated our very hearts."

"Were you frightened?"

"I am ashamed to say that I think we were all very afraid. I never imagined that I would see an angel before I left this life. But the angel told us to 'Fear not.' He told us that he brought 'good tidings of great joy, which shall be to all people.' Then he said that unto us 'is born this day in the city of David a Saviour, which is Christ the Lord.' He gave us a sign so that we would know the child. He said, 'Ye shall find the babe wrapped in swaddling clothes, lying in a manger.' "

"Was the manger that box thing He was lying in?"

"Yes, Jeshua. That box is a trough used to feed the animals in the stable. It is called a manger."

"I heard beautiful singing last night before I got up to your camp."

"Oh yes, after the angel had finished speaking to us, there appeared with him a multitude of the heavenly host. They sang praises to God. It was the most wonderful thing I ever heard! I shall never forget it. Nor should you, Jeshua."

After their meal, Eleazar and Jeshua worked until evening. Then Jeshua was sent down to the city to fetch another meal from Naomi.

As he made his way down the hillside, Jeshua reckoned

that it had been a very good day. He thought about Eleazar. The shepherd was getting older. Jeshua was but a young boy. Nevertheless he had been able to help Eleazar a great deal this day. Eleazar needed Jeshua's help, particularly during the busy lambing season. Perhaps, Jeshua thought, he should abandon his beggar's post by the city's gate and remain for a time with Eleazar in the hills.

He followed his nose to Naomi's house. The sweet smell of her cooking drew him down her street. She had already sent another pot of food to the stable, and so Jeshua was left without an excuse to visit the child and His family once more. A little disappointed, he picked up the pot Naomi gave him and climbed the path back to the shepherd's camp. The new star lit his way.

That night, as the shepherds sat by the fire, the talk again drifted to the occurrences of the night before. Jeshua Barnabas reflected on the young king's birth in that lowly stable. He now understood a little better that it must have been the will of God that the child be born in such circumstances, but Jeshua still felt bad for the newborn king. He had so little.

The child's family had been so kind. Jeshua wished that there were something he could do for them. Eleazar and the other shepherds had given the Messiah the firstlings of their flocks. Naomi had given the family the fruits of her hearth. Sadly, Jeshua was so very poor that he had neither a lamb to offer to the newborn king, nor even a crust of bread to give His family.

I saw the parents even before the child was born, he thought. *God must have put me in their way.*

"His family shall be my family," he whispered. "That is what His mother said. And she told me, 'It may be that He will need someone to watch over Him, to keep Him from any harm.'" A flush of pride crept again into Jeshua's cheeks. "She wants *me* to watch over Him!"

Then he sighed dejectedly. "Watch over him," he muttered. "I didn't even have a gift to give him on His birth." Jeshua thought of how little his few coins would buy. He had no means to honor the Holy One—tiny little Jeohua, the newborn King of the Jews, the Christ.

He fingered the leather strap that draped about his neck and held the small bag with all of his belongings. He looked down at the pouch and pursed his lips. He thought of the wooden lamb inside, and his face brightened. Perhaps he could carve a lamb for the child just as his father had carved this lamb for him!

Jeshua slipped away from the fire. None of the shepherds noticed his departure. He stood not far away, near a camp torch. He opened the pouch and withdrew the little lamb bequeathed him by his father. He could barely remember his father, but this little toy somehow bridged the divide between his father and him. It was the only thing Jeshua had that was especially his—made by a father for a young son whose mother had died giving him birth, a young son whose remaining parent would also leave him far too soon.

Jeshua gazed lovingly at the lamb. To him, it represented the most beautiful object he had ever seen. He marveled at the expert carving. The lamb looked so real. His father must have possessed much skill to carve such a thing. The light from the star played across the little figure, highlighting the lovely grain. The flame from the torch brought the warmth of the wood to the surface, the flickering almost sparking life into the toy.

Jeshua was so glad that he had such an object by which to remember his family. This was his entire inheritance— the only thing, other than life, bestowed him by his parents. As he often had before, he lifted the lamb to his lips and kissed it.

Then Jeshua thought of the lamb that he would carve for the child. Surely a wooden lamb would be an acceptable offering from a beggar boy who had no real lamb of his own to give. And the baby Jeshua would be able to play with a wooden lamb long before He would play with a real one. It would be a good gift! Maybe the child would even come to treasure His lamb as Jeshua did his own.

Jeshua happily imagined his next visit to the stable. On that visit, he would finally have a gift for the newborn king.

Chapter Five

And so, that very night, Jeshua borrowed Eleazar's cumbersome old knife and began carving any piece of wood he could find, with generally disastrous results. At first, he carved his fingers more than the bits of wood he was trying to shape, or so it seemed to him. Some pieces of hardwood completely rebuffed Eleazar's dull blade. Others split or splintered at the first cut. If he made any progress, he often found himself unintentionally cutting off the head or some other appendage of the lamb. This task was clearly going to be a little more difficult than Jeshua Barnabas had imagined.

The shepherds awakened before dawn, and Jeshua's days were heaped with the tasks of the lambing season. The work was often arduous and dirty. And the days grew warmer as the sun burned brighter, rising higher into the sky each day.

Jeshua's labor in the fields proved useful to Eleazar and to the other shepherds as well. He was always welcome in their midst. But the days were long, and exhaustion threatened to overcome Jeshua by day's end. Still, every night he fought off sleep and struggled to whittle his present for the Christ child.

Even though Jeshua made brief trips to Bethlehem, Naomi never again asked him to take a meal to the child's family. Jeshua thought it unlikely that Naomi had offered no more meals to the holy family. He wondered if perhaps Naomi took food to them herself. He wanted to see the family and the child again, but he was also glad, in a way, that he had no occasion to visit them. He wanted to have a gift the next time he visited the king.

Days slipped into weeks, almost without Jeshua's awareness. Each night he worked on carving the little toy lamb for the Christ child. At first, he had been aided by the light of the star, which arose each night with its fellows. But, with the passage of time, the star grew dimmer, and the skies grew overcast, so Jeshua had to rely more on the light of the fire to illuminate his efforts.

The shepherds sometimes inquired as to what Jeshua was attempting to carve, but he never confided in them. He was afraid they might think a wooden lamb a poor gift. Besides, he had quickly become aware that he didn't have a lot of skill at carving and he didn't want anyone to laugh at his crude attempts. However, when he finished a piece, he would ask the shepherds what they thought it was.

The shepherds were often amused at Jeshua's endeavors.

"It is a loaf of bread," replied a shepherd regarding one of Jeshua's earliest efforts.

"No, I think it is some kind of fruit. Yes, it is clearly a

date. Is it not a date, Jeshua?" queried another. The others snickered.

As his efforts improved, the shepherds became more serious in guessing what Jeshua was carving.

"Ah, that is no doubt a table—see the legs!"

"No, there is a head. It is surely a turtle!"

Jeshua was nothing if not tenacious. He sat carving by the campfire for hours. At the end, he often fell asleep in the middle of a cut. No one could fault him for a lack of effort. The shepherds' initial amusement eventually turned to pity. Whatever he was trying to carve, he was clearly having a very difficult time accomplishing it.

His labors finally produced more animal-like results. The shepherds tried to be helpful, guessing all manner of mythical animals and ferocious beasts. But no one guessed a lamb.

Finally, one of the shepherds lent Jeshua his knife, which was smaller, sharper, and more suitable for carving. The shepherd also showed the boy how to hone the knife to keep its edge. Another shepherd, possessed of some skill at whittling, taught Jeshua how to shape a piece of wood and explained which kinds of wood were better for carving. He helped Jeshua find dried pieces of fir, cypress, cedar, and olive wood. He explained how to orient the grain of the wood to provide support for the more delicate parts of the figure.

At last, Jeshua produced something that would pass for a lamb. All of the shepherds recognized it as a lamb and agreed that it was a very fine piece of work, indeed. But

Jeshua knew that it was merely a poor facsimile of the little lamb he kept tucked in his pouch. Still, it represented a good effort for a nine-year-old boy without much skill at wood-carving.

Jeshua didn't think that the babe would care that the lamb was a little misshapen. It would still be a nice toy for the infant, who didn't appear to have any toys. Besides, although Jeshua had not had a lot of experience with babies, he had noticed that they weren't too particular about what they chose for playthings. And Jeshua was sure that the child would understand that an orphan boy was far too poor to be able to provide a real lamb as a gift.

Proudly, Jeshua rubbed the little olive wood figure with oil and polished it with the hem of his tunic. He blew on it to dry it, oiled it again, and then polished it some more until it glistened. His gift was ready.

✳

That night, he made a detour from his frequent pilgrim-age to the home of Naomi and ran to the stable where the Messiah had been born. He skidded to a halt at the door-way. Save for a few animals, eating or chewing their cud, the stable was empty.

It had never occurred to Jeshua that the holy family might not stay in the stable. How long had it been since the birth? Days—no, weeks. Maybe as many as six weeks. His little shoulders sagged. He turned and slowly trudged from the door.

A middle-aged man with a torch had drawn a bucket of water and was carrying it to replenish an outside trough farther down the way. Jeshua recognized the man as one of the stable keepers and approached him.

"Sir, do you know where the family in the stable over there has gone?"

"Don't know, son. Since the census decree, we've had quite a few families who have stayed at the stables."

"But this family had a son born in the stable."

"Ah, the Galileans. Here, hold this," said the man as he thrust the torch at Jeshua and then splashed the bucket of water into the trough. "I think they found a kinsman to take them in."

Jeshua's face brightened a little. "So they are still in Bethlehem?"

"I don't think so. I believe the woman's days of purification are over. The last I had heard they were about to travel to Jerusalem to present the child at the temple and to make their sacrifices. That was a day or two ago."

The man retrieved his torch and held it up to get a better look at the boy. "You are Jeshua, the orphan boy, are you not? What have you to do with this Nazarene family?"

"I . . . I came the night of their son's birth. He and I share the same name. I have a gift for him."

The man regarded the boy. "I am sorry, Jeshua. I don't know that they will come back. They may stay in Jerusalem for a season. But they are from Nazareth. They will most likely return there." He shook his head. "Indeed, they may have already left Jerusalem for the north."

Jeshua nodded dejectedly at the man and then shuffled away. He sat down at a distance from the stable and took the pouch from around his neck. He had wrapped the little carved lamb in the same cloth with his own lamb. He pulled out his gift for the child and studied it. It shone, even in the near darkness of the stable area.

Jerusalem was not a long distance away. But it was such a big city. Even if the family were still there, Jeshua would never be able to find them. And Nazareth—he didn't even know where Nazareth was.

It was his own fault. He had been too clumsy. It had taken too long to carve the lamb. Then he began to cry. . . .

Chapter Six

As the days passed, young Jeshua often thought of the child and His family. The family had been kind to him. His heart ached that they had left before he could deliver his gift. *His mother said that I could be part of His family*, he recalled. *She bade me to watch over Him—to keep Him from any harm.* Jeshua shifted. *Watch over Him*, Jeshua recalled bitterly. *I never even checked on Him after that first night. And now they are gone.*

Jeshua reflected sadly that he most likely would never see the child or His family again. Jeshua remembered the love and adoration with which the mother had regarded her son. He was glad that the little Messiah was born into such a loving family. Jeshua longed for such a family. He had never known his own mother, and his father had died before Jeshua was five. He wished that his parents had lived a little longer. He sometimes felt so lonely. It was hard to be young and not have a family to take care of him. Eleazar and Naomi and the shepherds were kind to him, but Jeshua wished that he could have a real family, a family like the child's, a family to love him.

People yet gathered to Bethlehem and to other cities in Judaea for the census and taxation. The City of David continued to teem with strangers, although others had already paid their taxes and departed. The oppression of Rome and its minions was only too evident in the plague of officials and tax collectors sent to vex the little city's inhabitants. In his comings and goings, Jeshua dodged all manner of haughty administrators and mercenaries who tramped the streets of Bethlehem and were sometimes very harsh toward beggar boys. Worst, and most cruel, were the soldiers of Herod the Great. Many of them were Idumaeans, with little love for Judaeans. Herod's soldiers often slew individuals over a mere trifle. Jeshua hoped that the holy family was well beyond the reach of butchers like them.

Yet, with all of the people in Bethlehem, it was also a good time for begging. Most of the lambing was over, and Jeshua had abandoned the hills to beg in the streets again. He would sometimes eat at the home of Eleazar and Naomi but more often fended for himself. He suspected that Eleazar knew why Jeshua had carved the little lamb, but Eleazar never asked him about it. And Jeshua never told. He was ashamed that he had never been able to deliver his gift to the child who shared his name.

Jeshua frequently sat by the city gate in the late afternoons. As folks returned from the fields, they sometimes would spare a coin for a beggar boy. One particular day, Jeshua found his usual spot outside of the gate. In the warmth of the setting sun, Jeshua sat with his hand outstretched, his back against the city wall. His other hand clutched his leather pouch, and he idly fingered the outlines of the two little lambs bundled inside. His thoughts drifted again to the child—and the undelivered gift.

He barely noticed as a group of travelers, mostly women, made their way down the road and began filing through the gate. A portly woman paused and dropped a coin into Jeshua's hand.

"Peace be unto you, young Jeshua."

Jeshua started and replied, "And unto you, my mistress." He recognized the voice of Shapira, widow of the old baker. He had occasionally run errands for her.

"My dear, perhaps you should pay better attention to your begging."

Jeshua glanced at the small bronze coin, a lepton, in his palm. "Many thanks, and a blessing be upon you, my mistress."

"I also purchased some dates at the market in Jerusalem. Here are three for you, my dear. They are from Bethany, and very sweet."

Jeshua eagerly accepted the dates. "Thank you! Thank you, my mistress!"

Shapira's companions had halted and were waiting for her. "You are welcome, Jeshua. I hope that you enjoy them." She turned to move on.

"Were you in Jerusalem long, my mistress?"

Shapira again looked down at Jeshua. "Not long, my dear. We left yesterday and spent the night at the house of my sister and her husband." She tilted her head, peering at the guards of the gate, who had meandered off toward the bazaar down the road. "The Holy City is very busy. And, as everywhere, it is filled with many foreigners."

"Was there any news, my mistress?" asked Jeshua, wondering if perhaps there might be word of the coronation of a new king.

"It is strange that you should ask, Jeshua. There were tidings at the temple." She lowered her voice and leaned closer to Jeshua. "It is said that a holy man named Simeon and the aged prophetess, Anna, daughter of Phanuel—she a remarkable woman who has fasted and prayed at the temple for, lo, longer than I have lived—greeted an infant in the courtyards of the temple some days ago and declared Him to be the Anointed One. People say that it had been revealed to the good Simeon 'that he should not see death, before he had seen the Lord's Christ.' "

Jeshua caught his breath. This was surely the child!

Shapira glanced again at the guards down the way. "Pray that old villain, Herod, does not hear of this young Messiah," she whispered.

"Was there word of where the child has gone?" Jeshua inquired hopefully.

"No one knows. It is rumored they were Galileans." One of the women in Shapira's group beckoned. "I must go, my dear. Peace be unto you, Jeshua. Enjoy the dates."

"And unto you, my mistress. I shall, and thank you."

Jeshua pondered this news. The stable keeper had said that the family had gone to present the child at the temple.

It must be that He was the infant spoken of by Shapira. But His whereabouts were still unknown. Jeshua's gift would remain undelivered.

Jeshua sighed, realizing how very hungry he was. He greedily devoured the dates Shapira had given him, but the three dates did not satiate his hunger. He continued to suck on the pits to calm the rumblings in his stomach.

The sun disappeared behind the hills, and twilight slowly stole away. The sky was clear as the stars winked into view. The great star had reappeared and shone almost as brightly as it had that first night. Jeshua looked for the guards of the gate. They lingered a distance away, having found some beverage to imbibe, and now appeared embroiled in a heated argument. The gate should have been closed. The guards were neglecting their duty. *No matter,* thought Jeshua. He had nowhere to go. He was enjoying sitting where he was. He found it pleasant to gaze upon the star.

A whisper of a breeze swept from the north, and Jeshua raised his head. He thought he had heard something. He strained his keen ears to hear. There. He had not been mistaken. The breeze carried the sound of bells and the braying of camels.

By the light of the star, he could see all the way to where the road from Jerusalem emerged from the hills. Slowly, shadows materialized in the distance. It was a caravan! Few came by way of Bethlehem, but this was definitely one of those rare companies that would pass through.

The caravan didn't appear to be very large. Most likely it had stopped in Jerusalem and was now traveling south.

But it was late, and the company might choose to spend the night near or in the city.

Jeshua arose and ran down the road. Any caravan certainly warranted further investigation. He intercepted the vanguard of the procession while it yet remained a distance from the city. Surveying the bearing and raiment of the retinue, Jeshua concluded that this was not a merchant caravan. This was an entourage for persons of rank. Perhaps there were alms to be had!

Jeshua scanned the first few members of the train. Then he spotted a turbaned youth, several years his senior, walking some distance before one of the camels. With the aplomb of years of begging, Jeshua sidled up to the young man, ignoring his waves of dismissal.

"Greetings, my master," began Jeshua, bowing and touching his fingers to his forehead. "Whence comest thou?"

"Begone, boy!" came the haughty reply. The language was foreign, but not so different that Jeshua couldn't understand the words, particularly in light of the curt gesture that accompanied the dismissal.

"A thousand pardons!" responded Jeshua with one of the phrases he had learned from the older beggars. He bowed again. "Perhaps I may later be of service when the evening chores are to be done?"

This inquiry apparently interested the older youth. He still regarded the beggar boy disdainfully, but said, "Perhaps—if thou wilt keep from under foot!"

Jeshua smiled. He was meeting with success more

quickly than he had hoped. He was still curious, however, and again bowed low. "Hast thou journeyed long, my master?" He glanced out of the corner of his eye and saw that his obeisance was having the desired effect.

"We come today from Jerusalem," the youth replied importantly. "From the palace of Herod the Great!"

Ah, thought Jeshua, *these are surely persons of great rank, to have been entertained by King Herod, himself.* Jeshua again addressed the older boy, "And what lords dost thou serve?"

"They are eminent sages, nobles of venerated houses. They are the wisest men of our land." The youth turned toward Jeshua and commanded imperiously, "See that thou dost stay well out of their way!"

Jeshua inclined his head in acknowledgement. "And where is the land of these wise men?" he pressed.

"We have traveled far over many days . . . ," began the youth.

"Aram, does the boy seek alms?" queried a deep voice from atop a camel that had moved closer.

Startled, Jeshua whirled around. Somewhat apprehensively, he raised his eyes to the imposing figure who had ridden up behind. Judging by the person's rich raiment and the costly trappings of his mount, this was likely one of the wise men, a person of high rank. Jeshua had not had many experiences with such persons, and nearly all of those experiences had been bad. Such people were generally not kind to beggars. Had not this boy, Aram, just warned him to stay out of the way of these sages? Yet here he was, with one of them only feet away!

Chapter Seven

Aram had turned, fallen to his knees, and now pressed his forehead to the ground. Jeshua speedily followed his example.

"My lord Gushnasaph." Aram cleared his throat. "Excellency, this boy was . . . ," he began.

Jeshua intuitively decided that he would fare better if *he* responded instead of Aram. This man clearly possessed great authority, but he also sounded kind. Jeshua took the chance. Still on his knees, Jeshua raised his head and, without making eye contact, quickly said, "Peace be unto you, my lord." He touched his hand to his forehead and bowed low again. "I was merely asking whence came this caravan, my lord," continued Jeshua. Aram remained bowed but looked askance at Jeshua, obviously annoyed at being interrupted.

"And peace be unto thee, my son," replied the man, his face still hidden in the darkness. His words were now in an accented but well-spoken and more familiar dialect of Aramaic, no doubt to make the conversation easier for Jeshua.

His voice remained gentle. "Please, arise." Aram rose and stood waiting attentively. Jeshua did likewise. "We journey from a land to the east," the man said. He studied Jeshua. "Art thou of Bethlehem?"

"I . . . I am, indeed, my lord. It is the city of my birth." Jeshua kept his eyes averted.

"We are come into this land seeking Him who is born King of the Jews. Hast thou perchance heard of His birth?"

Jeshua froze. Idle curiosity, food, begging—suddenly none of these were of any consequence. His heart pounded. "Sire, is the king ye seek the Deliverer, the newborn Messiah?"

The man signaled, and everyone behind halted. All eyes were now upon the beggar boy. "Thy king and the chief priests and scribes of this land have called Him the Christ," the man said. "He is, in truth, the one we seek. We saw His star and have journeyed far to worship Him."

"My . . . my lord," stammered Jeshua, "I visited the babe the night of His birth, the night the new star appeared."

There was a moment's pause. The man tapped a crop to the camel, and the animal rocked to and fro as it descended to the ground. Those nearby in the entourage scurried to assist the man in dismounting. Accompanied by a torch-bearer, he approached Jeshua, who drew back, now completely forsaken by his beggar's bravado.

Jeshua cast a quick glance at Aram, who had stepped deferentially aside as the Magus approached. Aram offered no help but currently regarded the beggar boy with heightened interest.

"Thou hast nothing to fear, my son," Lord Gushnasaph said kindly. "What is thy name?"

"Jeshua. Jeshua Barnabas, my lord," Jeshua replied hesitantly, still looking at the ground.

"Jeshua, the night of the babe's birth, how didst thou know that the child was the Anointed One?"

"A—Angels, my lord." Jeshua looked warily at all of those who had surrounded him. "Angels heralded His birth, that night of the star, to certain shepherds in the fields, and told them where to find the babe."

"Angels," repeated the Magus softly. "Didst thou see these angels, Jeshua?"

"No, my lord. But the shepherds saw them." For the first time, Jeshua hazarded a peek at the face of the wise man, who bore benevolent features but continued to study Jeshua intently. "I . . . I did hear the angels, my lord," Jeshua added.

"Thou didst hear the angels, Jeshua?" asked the wise man.

"I heard them sing, my lord. I have never heard anything more beautiful. I was not there when they spoke to the shepherds. But I did go with the shepherds that night to see the newborn king. His name is Jeshua. He has the same name as I."

The other Magi had now ridden near. Lord Gushnasaph turned and addressed the others. "My Lords Hormisdas and Larvandad, this lad is young Master Jeshua Barnabas, of Bethlehem. He has visited the new King of the Jews. He was there the night of the child's birth."

Jeshua turned toward the other Magi and prostrated himself on the ground. The other Magi each greeted him, saying, "Peace be unto thee, oh Jeshua of Bethlehem."

"And unto you, my lords," Jeshua replied meekly.

Lord Gushnasaph bade Jeshua arise. He put a hand on the boy's shoulders and looked into his face.

"Jeshua Barnabas," began the wise man. "We are come to worship Him who is born King of the Jews. We do not seek to harm Him. Dost thou know where we might find Him?"

"I do not, my lord." Jeshua's lip quivered. "I wish I knew. I . . ." Jeshua bowed his head. "I have a gift for Him but have not seen Him since that first night." His voice broke. "The child's mother told me to watch over Him, but I do not know where to find Him. I have not been able to give Him my gift."

Lord Gushnasaph lifted Jeshua's chin with his hand. By the light of the star, Jeshua could see the wise man's eyes searching his own.

"Jeshua Barnabas, we also bring gifts for the child. We have just sought Him at the court of thy ruler, His Royal Highness, King Herod, who directed us here to Bethlehem, the city of the prophecy."

"He was surely born in Bethlehem, my lord," said Jeshua. "But I heard that His family took Him to Jerusalem, to present Him at the temple. I do not know where they went after. His family is Galilean."

Jeshua abruptly knelt again before the Magus and touched his forehead to the ground. "Please, Sire, I beg of you. If ye seek the child in Galilee, may I go with you, that I may deliver my gift to Him?"

The wise man reached down and helped Jeshua to his feet. "My son, I perceive that the same spirit which has touched us concerning this child has touched thee as well. Of course thou mayest accompany us. But look—the star, which has again appeared tonight, has not pointed to Galilee but has led us here to Bethlehem, even as the chief priests and scribes of King Herod's court have indicated."

Bethlehem. Jeshua's own city. Was it possible that the child had returned here? His pulse raced. He should have searched, made more inquiries. But his heart leapt with hope that the babe may have come back to Bethlehem. At last, Jeshua might deliver the gift that he had spent so many days preparing.

"Oh, sire," Jeshua cried, "I would be so grateful if I should be permitted to go with you to find the new king."

The wise man patted Jeshua on the back. "And so thou shalt, my son. So thou shalt. Look, the star stands even now over thy city of Bethlehem. Let us go and see if the City of David yet shelters the heir to the throne of David."

Chapter Eight

And so, Jeshua, the beggar boy, accompanied the wise
men and their retinue into the city of Bethlehem.

Despite the evening hour, the entrance of the caravan
into the small city drew considerable attention. A crowd
gathered to follow the procession as it coursed through the
narrow streets toward a house that appeared to be bathed
most particularly in the light of the star. Jeshua walked with
Lord Gushnasaph, who had remained on foot. An attendant
led the camel, who brayed disapprovingly at the clusters of
people now lining the streets. Some recognized Jeshua and
were astonished to see him walking side by side with one of
the eastern Magi. Jeshua blushed when he saw several in the
crowd pointing at him.

As the entourage passed the street where Eleazar and
Naomi lived, Jeshua suddenly wondered if the old shepherd
were in the hills tonight. If he were not, Eleazar would surely
want to know about the wise men and to see the Christ
Child once again. Naomi would want to see the family as

well. Jeshua spoke to the wise man and begged leave to run to their home.

"He is an old shepherd who was there that first night. He saw the angels. His wife knows the family. If they are home, I will bring them also to see the child. We will catch up to my lord's caravan."

"Very well, Jeshua." The Magus smiled. "With this crowd, it should not be too hard to find us."

Eleazar was indeed home and most eager to accompany Jeshua to see these Magi who had come to visit the child.

"Imagine—they have traveled so far to see our little king!" exclaimed Eleazar. "They saw His star all the way in the East, you say, Jeshua? What wonders cannot our God perform?"

Gentle Naomi also wanted to go with Jeshua and her husband. She, of course, wanted to see the Magi, but she also wanted to visit the family again.

"These Magi think the babe is still in Bethlehem?" asked Naomi. "We've certainly heard nothing about Him. Wouldn't we have heard if the family were still here, Eleazar?"

"Perhaps they didn't want anyone to know, Naomi."

"Perhaps. But it is odd," said Naomi. "They were very friendly toward us. As I've told Eleazar, Jeshua, after that first night, while you were in the fields, I went to the stable a number of times. I took the family food and things to make them more comfortable, you know. They had so little." She sighed.

"I think they finally did locate a distant kinsman, but I

never heard if they moved in with him or not," she continued. "I knew that the little mother was soon to complete her days of purification. . . . Her name was Maryam, you remember. So I imagined that they would be going to Jerusalem to present the child at the temple. But I never heard a word about them coming back here. I just thought they would go back to Nazareth. They were Nazarenes, you recall. If these wise men are right, and the family is still here, it's so strange we didn't know."

"It is said by some that Herod's spies here in the city may have heard rumors of the birth of the Savior. That child is not safe as long as that scoundrel, Herod, is on the throne," said Eleazar.

Naomi looked alarmed and pulled the shutter more tightly on the window. "Eleazar, be careful! Your voice might be heard in the street!"

"Well, it's true," replied Eleazar. "The old fox will not tolerate a new king. The child's parents surely know this. If they did come back to Bethlehem, they no doubt have been in hiding."

Eleazar noticed Jeshua glancing toward the door. "Come, Naomi. Jeshua awaits. We should not tarry. The Lord has brought these wise men to our little city. We must go and see if they have found our young deliverer."

Eleazar and Naomi tended to move slowly, but Jeshua gently hurried them as much as he could. He guided them though several alleys, which formed a shortcut to where the caravan of the Magi had been headed. Ahead, they could hear the noise of the crowd.

Jeshua slowed his pace. He turned to the elderly couple. "The wise men have brought gifts for the king," he said. He hesitated. "Eleazar, that little lamb that I carved—that was to be my gift for the Christ Child."

"And a handsome gift it would be, Jeshua!" cried Eleazar, panting as he caught up to the orphan boy.

"Do you think so?' asked Jeshua.

"Oh yes, Jeshua. You did a fine job on that lamb," Eleazar replied. "Naomi, you should see the clever carving Jeshua did while we were in the fields."

"Do you think I should give it to the child?"

"Of course, Jeshua. He will think it a fine gift indeed." Eleazar smiled. "When He gets a little older, of course!"

Jeshua grinned happily. If the child really was still in Bethlehem, Jeshua would finally be able to deliver his gift.

They caught up to the caravan just as it arrived at the house that had reflected the light of the star. The crowd had become much larger and now completely surrounded the caravan, spilling into the surrounding streets. Jeshua clambered to the top of a courtyard wall to see above the crowd. He watched as a servant was dispatched to the door of the home to make inquiries. When the servant turned and gave a nod of affirmation, the other wise men dismounted and attendants scurried to unload certain items from the baggage. Other servants, using dusters, hovered around the three and frantically began removing the grime of the road from the robes of the Magi.

Jeshua jumped down and attempted to guide Eleazar and Naomi through the press of people, but to little avail.

The crowd was not disposed to surrender position to an orphan boy escorting an elderly couple.

"Please, let us through!" pleaded Jeshua. But the people paid him little heed. "Please, we must get through!" Several in the crowd turned, annoyed, and waved away the beggar boy.

At the opposite end of the crowd, Aram, arrayed with the other servants in a line to keep the townspeople at a respectful distance, turned toward the plaintive cries The turbaned youth glanced at the Magi and then left the entourage, plunging through the crowd to Jeshua and his friends. Aram gave Jeshua and the elderly couple a curt nod. "Pray come with me," he said. He motioned for Jeshua and the couple to link hands with his and, in a loud, imperative voice, cried, "Make way! Make way!" The crowd parted for Aram, and he was able to escort Jeshua, Eleazar, and Naomi through the throng of people.

Hearing Aram's approach, Lord Gushnasaph turned and nodded to the youth and then smiled at Jeshua. "Ah, Jeshua, are these the two of whom thou didst speak?" he inquired. He gestured to the other wise men. "My lords, young master Jeshua has returned with his friends. They are also acquainted with the family of the child. Jeshua, pray introduce us to this goodly couple."

Jeshua heard the murmurings of astonishment by the townspeople at the attention accorded to one of the city's orphan boys by this great lord. With just a little more show than would normally be required, Jeshua introduced Eleazar and Naomi to the wise men, who received them graciously.

Eleazar awkwardly bowed and Naomi curtsied. Both appeared overwhelmed to be in the presence of these august lords.

"Our servants have inquired and tell us the child is here in this dwelling," continued Lord Gushnasaph. He searched the faces of the beggar boy, and the shepherd and his wife. "My brethren have wondered if this house is indeed where the child was born. The abode seems, ah, more humble than one would envisage for the King of the Jews. Surely a palace would serve as a more seemly residence for a king."

When Eleazar and Naomi hesitated to respond, Jeshua spoke. "My lords, the child was born in a stable on the outskirts of town."

"A stable?" asked Lord Hormisdas. "Would the One God have allowed the King of the Jews to be born in a stable?"

"My lords," began Eleazar quietly. "I was in the fields the night the star first appeared. I saw the angel of the Lord. He told us that he brought us 'good tidings of great joy, which shall be to all people,' and said that unto us was born that 'day in the city of David a Saviour, which is Christ the Lord.' Then there appeared a multitude of the heavenly host. They praised God and proclaimed, 'Glory to God in the highest, and on earth peace, good will toward men.' "

"Were there others who saw these things?" asked Lord Hormisdas.

"There were, my lord. My fellow shepherds all witnessed these events," replied Eleazar.

"And thou and the shepherds did visit the child?"

"Yea, my lord. The angel said that a sign unto us would be that we should 'find the babe wrapped in swaddling clothes, lying in a manger.' And so He was when we found Him that night. Young Jeshua was with us. And my wife, Naomi, later visited the family. God willed that He be born in a stable. But He is the king. More, He is the Christ! This I know."

"The account good Eleazar gives is most compelling, my lords," said Lord Gushnasaph. "The events he describes must have happened the very night that we first saw the star. No less than angels announced the birth. The child was born here in Bethlehem as the priests and scribes of King Herod said He would. And the star has led us to this very house. Can there be any doubt?"

The other two wise men agreed. "There can be no doubt. Let us enter and pay homage to the young king."

The other Magi prepared to enter the home. Lord Gushnasaph beckoned Eleazar and Naomi to follow. He put his hand on Jeshua's shoulder and leaned down to speak in the boy's ear. His voice resonated with anticipation.

"Come, Jeshua, let us see if we have finally found Him whom we seek."

Chapter Nine

*J*eshua entered the home behind the wise man and just before Eleazar and Naomi. As he passed the doorpost, Eleazar whispered from behind, "Jeshua, don't forget the mezuzah!" Looking up to the right of the door, Jeshua saw the case for the scroll of scriptures that God had commanded be placed on the doorposts of all homes. Eleazar and Naomi had taught him many of the customs of his people. He touched the mezuzah with two of his fingertips, which he then kissed. He bowed his head and recited the prayer: "May God protect my going out and coming in, now and forever."

As Jeshua crossed the threshold of the home, before he ever saw who was in the room, he felt the same warmth he had felt on that first holy night. He *knew* the Christ child was there. Sure enough, at the far end of the room sat Joseph and Maryam. And there was the babe, held by Maryam on her lap. Around them scurried a few of their kin, who appeared stunned at the entrance of these great eastern lords.

Jeshua sidled up to Lord Gushnasaph, who was just

ahead, and gestured toward the child. "That is the newborn king, my lord." The Magus nodded.

As much of the multitude from outside as could be accommodated pushed into the room after the Magi's party had entered. The crowd lined the walls.

It was Joseph who arose, at the urging of his kinsman, and somewhat hesitantly came forward to greet the Magi. He inclined his head courteously, saying, "May peace be unto you, my lords."

"And unto thee, thou son of David," replied Lord Hormisdas with a slight bow. He indicated the other wise men. "These are my lords Larvandad and Gushnasaph. I am Hormisdas. We have traveled far, seeking Him who is born King of the Jews, for we have seen His star in the East and are come to worship Him."

Joseph glanced at Maryam and his kin. He again bowed his head. "I am Joseph Bar-Heli." Motioning toward the back of the room, he continued. "This is my wife, Maryam. And this is the noble Toma, my kinsman, and his wife, Tabitha. This is their home."

Toma and Tabitha, with their children collected behind them, nervously greeted the great lords. Joseph then reverently swept his hand toward the child. "And, finally, my lords, I believe this is He whom ye seek. He is, indeed, heir to the throne of David. We were commanded to call Him Jeshua."

"Jeshua," Lord Larvandad repeated. *The Lord Saveth.*

Lord Hormisdas studied the child. "His lineage then is certain?" he asked.

"It is," replied Joseph. "My wife and I are both descended

of the house of Judah and are of the royal Davidic line. We trace our ancestry back here to Bethlehem, city of our fathers and the birthplace of King David himself." He paused. "Moreover, the angel Gabriel appeared to the child's mother before His birth. The angel declared that 'He shall be great, and shall be called the Son of the Highest: and the Lord God shall give unto him the throne of his father David; And he shall reign over the house of Jacob for ever; and of his kingdom there shall be no end.' "

The wise man swallowed hard. "The angel Gabriel," Lord Hormisdas repeated softly. He shook his head. With a touch of awe in his voice, and a new deference, he addressed the holy parents. "Forgive me, my lord and lady, children of David. I was wrong even to question the child's lineage." He turned to the other two wise men with an expression of astonishment. "These reports of angelic visitors are most singular. A star in the heavens, hosts of angels, and even one of the greatest of those angels, Gabriel, have heralded this infant's birth. What manner of child is this?" He hesitated, apparently weighing the import of his next words. "This is no ordinary king. Can He truly be the Anointed One of Jewish scripture?"

Lord Larvandad's eyes betrayed his own astonishment. "The angel Gabriel called Him 'the Son of the Highest'?" Joseph silently nodded. Lord Larvandad looked at the infant with wonder. "I too believe that this child must be much more than a king of the Jews. His own people and even angels have called Him 'Christ, the Lord.' If He is the Messiah, did not the ancient prophet foretell that He shall also be called *Emmanuel?*" Lowering his voice, he averred, *"God with us."*

Lord Gushnasaph smiled benevolently at the holy family. He glanced from one to the other of his fellow wise men and reverently declared, "The holy writ lists many titles He shall bear. And He is worthy of each of them. The Spirit hath borne witness to me that He is certainly the One. He is Lord of us all. Come, my lords, let us worship Him whom God hath sent."

To the amazement of the townspeople present, the noble lords fell to their knees and worshipped the child. Jeshua, Eleazar, and Naomi, as well as some of those watching, followed the example of the wise men.

The Magi then signaled for their treasures to be brought forth. To Lord Hormisdas was handed an object wrapped in fine cloth. The wise man unwrapped the gift, revealing a splendid chest adorned with glistening jewels. He approached the child and knelt, holding the chest in both hands. Slowly, he unlatched the chest and pulled back the lid, exposing the contents, which appeared to be pure gold. The gold caught the light of the lamps and flung it into the disbelieving eyes of those assembled against the walls of the room. Collectively, the crowd drew in its breath.

Lord Hormisdas set the chest before the child. "For the *King of Kings*," he said. Then he bowed his head to the floor.

Lord Hormisdas withdrew, and Lord Larvandad approached the child. He carefully unwrapped an alabaster jar. He removed the lid and the sweet aroma of frankincense filled the room. A murmur ran through the crowd.

The wise man placed the jar before the child. "For the *Prince of Peace*," he proclaimed, and then he also bowed to the ground.

As Lord Larvandad withdrew, Lord Gushnasaph approached. He unwrapped another costly container, inlaid with such fiery jewels that the onlookers gasped. As he opened the vessel, the fragrance of myrrh spilled across the room.

Offering his gift to the child, the third wise man declared in a hushed tone, "For the *Redeemer of us all.*" Many in the crowd looked at each other. Awed silence accompanied the wise man's obeisance to the Lord.

After several moments, Lord Gushnasaph arose. He looked around at Jeshua and then said to the holy family, "I have a young friend who has also brought a gift for the child. His name, like the child's, is Jeshua. I believe that your paths may have previously crossed."

The frigid grip of panic suddenly clenched Jeshua Barnabas's young heart. He had been enjoying the proceedings until now. But he had also imagined that he would bestow his gift in private, after all had left. He had not anticipated conferring his gift in front of the Magi and all of these people.

He gazed miserably at the resplendent offerings of the Magi. How could his poor gift compete with these? What was he to do? How could he stop this? He searched for something to say.

The wise man gently motioned for Jeshua to come forward. Joseph and Maryam both smiled at the boy. He crept slowly out of the crowd. As the people recognized him, titters spread from the peripheries of the room. Jeshua's face burned with shame. He wildly cast around him for a means of escape. Then he looked again at the child's parents. Maryam perceived his discomfort.

"Jeshua! How nice to see you again!" She nodded at him. Her smile was warm, genuine, and the laughter in the room subsided. She briefly looked beyond Jeshua and nodded as well to Naomi and Eleazar, who remained at the far end of the room. Then she beckoned Jeshua to come closer.

Jeshua cast about the room. Many of the townspeople smirked, but Eleazar and Naomi signaled for him to go on. He hung his head and timidly stepped into the middle of the room. Lord Gushnasaph put his arm around Jeshua and directed him closer to the child. "It is all right, Jeshua," he said. "Do not be afraid."

Jeshua peeked into the wise man's kind eyes. *He surely does not know how poor is my gift*, thought Jeshua. He reflected bitterly that it had been a great mistake to think that he, an insignificant beggar boy, could offer any gift of use or consequence to the young king. He felt the amused stares of the gawking townspeople bore into him from behind. Perspiration dampened his brow, and he fought back hot tears.

He took a step forward and once again thought of bolting from the room. Running would at least save him from the embarrassment that was coming. His exit would be a good joke for all the townspeople to tell tomorrow, but it would soon be forgotten. He glanced back at the door. Then Lord Gushnasaph, sensing Jeshua's great fear, returned to his side. The noble lord gently raised Jeshua's chin and scanned his face. "Jeshua, thou hast nothing to fear," the Magus repeated softly. "Pay no heed to the crowd. The child's parents are thy friends."

Then the wise man guided Jeshua's gaze toward Maryam and Joseph. Jeshua was only a poor orphan, but the couple from Nazareth looked at him almost as if he were one of the Magi. He felt the wise man behind him withdraw. Jeshua could not look away from the countenances of the holy parents. While derision tarnished the expressions of many in the room, love flowed from Joseph's and Maryam's eyes.

He swallowed and then slowly reached down, removed the pouch from his tunic, and pulled the cord over his head. He opened the pouch and carefully unwrapped the little wooden sheep. It was as though tonight he was seeing the little lamb he had carved for the very first time. Tonight he saw it in the cold light of reality. It looked like a nine-year-old had carved it. No, it looked like a *four-year-old* had carved it. He held in his hand a misshapen bit of wood that bore only the slightest resemblance to a lamb. He looked again at the beautiful gifts of the Magi and then back at his poor attempt to carve a lamb.

Words of apology had crept to his lips when he became aware of another pair of eyes regarding him. They were the child's. The newborn king was but an infant, but Jeshua met the child's gaze with affection. They shared the same name, after all.

Hadn't Eleazar once told Jeshua that his name meant *The Lord Saveth*? Hadn't one of the wise men this night affirmed that same meaning? For the beggar boy, it was only a name. But for this child—He *was* the Savior whom God had sent.

Jeshua tenderly contemplated the young king. The infant's family had been kind to him, and His mother had said that the child's family would be *his* family. Jeshua felt a kinship with this family and with the young Savior. He didn't really know what the Savior's mission would be or how He would accomplish it, but Jeshua instinctively knew that, not only had the babe come for all the world, He had also come for Jeshua Barnabas, the beggar boy. The newborn king would make everything right.

Through Jeshua's tears, he thought he saw the child smile at him. Jeshua smiled back. Love was not an emotion with which Jeshua was well acquainted, but he felt love, the purest of love, fill his heart.

He looked again at the pitiful little lamb that he had carved. Alas, this was no gift for the Savior of the World. The other lamb was still partially wrapped in the bit of cloth. Jeshua's eye fell on it—the beautiful lamb his father had carved for him. His lip trembled. That little lamb meant the world to him. It was his most precious possession. It was his only remaining link with his family. But it would make a wonderful gift for the young child.

Tears now streamed down his face; he could not stop them. Slowly he raised his father's lamb to his lips and gave the figure a last kiss. His eyes again met the infant's. A warmth filled Jeshua's soul. In one hand he secreted the poor little piece of wood that he had carved for the child. In the other hand, he cradled the splendid lamb his father had made for him, his esteemed legacy. And it was his father's lamb that he very gently placed in the hands of little Jeshua, whom the world would come to know as Jesus, the Christ.

"For the *Lamb of God*," he whispered.

Chapter Ten

Many—too many—now knew of the newborn king. The wise men would be warned in a dream not to return to Herod. The flight of Jesus and His family into Egypt awaited the wee hours of the morrow. But tonight the holy family slept. During the night, an angel would appear to Joseph in a dream and command him to leave Bethlehem, to leave Judaea, to flee for the child's life.

Still, the babe slept blissfully, a little smile playing across His peaceful face. The gifts of the Magi sat on a table by the crib. The shimmering moonlight poured through an open window, tumbling off the gold and jewels of the price-less gifts, and erupting into a legion of muted colors that washed across the room. A gentle breeze stirred an open curtain and wafted the faint perfume of frankincense and myrrh across the slumbering infant.

The child stirred in His bed, bathed in the effulgence of those royal tokens brought by wise men from the East in adoration of Him who was heir to the scepter of Judah, rightful King of the Jews. But the gift He clutched close to His heart in His repose that night was another gift—the fourth gift—a little hand-carved figure of a lamb, the precious gift of a beggar boy.

Postscript

For younger readers, this story perhaps is finished. But the narrative is based on a much more important history, and some readers may yet entertain questions about certain elements of the Nativity story itself.

While many modern Christmas tales deal with contemporary themes of the season, I wanted *The Fourth Gift* to return to why we celebrate the holiday. Christmas is, of course, the commemoration of the birth of Christ, a fact sometimes obscured by the trendy trappings of the season.

The idea of a little beggar boy who eventually gives his most precious possession to the infant Jesus appealed to me because that same Jesus would ultimately surrender all that He had, including His very life, to atone for each of us. And our Heavenly Father, who gave the world His Only Begotten Son, certainly bestowed upon us His most precious possession. Through the birth of Christ, the world is to receive its salvation—a priceless gift—one beyond comprehension. This, it seems to me, is the true meaning of Christmas and the reason Christmas is the holiday of joy, good will, and generosity.

The Fourth Gift is obviously a work of fiction, but the story is based on events that many of us regard as sacred. I have therefore tried to be faithful to both the scriptural account and the historic context of that first Christmas, keeping in mind the traditions of many Christian faiths. The scriptural record is silent on many details, so I have attempted to extrapolate from the original accounts as carefully as possible. However, there may be a number of details in the story that appear new to readers or differ from popular accounts of the Nativity. Consequently, I thought an explanation of some of those details might be in order.

The language believed to have been spoken commonly by the Jews at the time of Jesus was Aramaic.[1] This ancient Semitic language was used or adopted by a number of the great pre-Christian Middle Eastern kingdoms and empires.[2] Aramaic apparently replaced the earlier Hebrew after the Jews returned from their captivity in Babylon.[3] While Christ's native tongue would most likely have been Aramaic, he might also have been conversant in Greek (much of the eastern Mediterranean had been Hellenized) and, as a Jewish teacher, he was probably fluent in Hebrew, as well.[4] Depending on the occasion, he may have taught in each of these languages.

Jeshua[5] (it is often rendered *Yeshua*[6] in Hebrew[7]) is therefore an anglicized form of the Aramaic name that Christ most likely bore, although some authorities prefer *Yeshua* as the anglicized Aramaic form.[8] The meaning of the name is often translated as "the Lord saveth," "God is help,"[9] "Jehovah is salvation,"[10] or sometimes just "Savior."[11] It is a late contracted form of the earlier *Jehoshua*[12] (in Hebrew, *Yehoshua*[13] or *Yehowshua*,[14] among other variations) or *Joshua*,[15] meaning "God is help" or "help of Jehovah."[16] We, of course, are more familiar with the name *Jesus*, which is the English version of the Greek *Iēsoûs*[17] (Ἰησοῦς[18]). *Jesus* is the name that appears in the Bible because the Gospel accounts were widely circulated in Greek. *Christ* is a title, derived from *Christōs* (Χριστός),[19] the Greek word for the Hebrew term, *Messiah*.[20] It means "the anointed"[21] or "the Anointed One."[22]

Jeshua (or *Yeshua*) was probably a common boy's name;[23] hence, it is also the name of the beggar boy in the story. I hoped using Aramaic names would give a more authentic feel to the story. Having the beggar boy share the same name as Jesus is obviously a device to strengthen the bond that the beggar boy feels toward the infant Jesus. The orphan's surname is *Barnabas*, meaning "son of consolation" or sometimes "son of exhortation."[24] *Bar* is an Aramaic prefix that denotes "son of" (the Hebrew equivalent is *Ben*).[25]

Shapira is an Aramaic name that means "good." *Toma*, a form of Thomas, means "twin," and *Tabitha* means "gazelle."[26] There are no easily recognizable English-Aramaic equivalents for most of the other biblical names in the story, with the exception of *Mary*. *Maryam* is the anglicized Aramaic version of *Mary*[27] and the form I use in the story. The Hebrew version is often written *Miryam* or *Miriam*.[28]

In chapter 2 of the story, Joseph introduces himself to the shepherds as "Joseph Bar-Heli, of Nazareth." The Gospels of Matthew (Matthew 1:1–16) and Luke (Luke 3:23–38) chronicle two different genealogies of Christ. Both genealogies go through Joseph, Christ's apparent and legal father. However, the father of Joseph differs in each account. Matthew lists Jacob as Joseph's father (Matthew 1:16), whereas Luke states that Joseph's father is Heli (Luke 3:23). The genealogies differ in other respects as well, although both assert descent through King David and Abraham, with only Luke carrying the line all the way back to Adam.

Some authorities suggest that one of the genealogies is that of Joseph and the other is Mary's.[29] Under that premise, one of the fathers of Joseph listed would actually be Joseph's father by marriage. Joseph and Mary were likely cousins, and both were of the royal blood of the House of David, so naturally the genealogies would be very similar.[30]

Other authorities maintain that Matthew's account details the royal and legal descent by which Joseph and hence Christ would have claimed the throne of Israel, while Luke's version catalogs the actual biological descent of Joseph.[31] In the story, I have adopted this latter theory and made Heli the father of Joseph.

Apart from the characters' names, I have also adopted other conventions. In many languages, and presumably in the Aramaic of Christ's time, the familiar form of the second person personal pronoun ("thou") is used among family or to address children or close friends. In English, terms such as "thou" have fallen out of use and sound archaic. In the story, I limit the familiar form ("thou") to the conversations of the Magi and Aram, in order to give their speech a more exotic feel. Jeshua uses the familiar "thou" in speaking to Aram, a boy, but the more formal "ye" (nominative case) or "you" (objective case) in speaking to the Magi, his elders.

Where possible, I have attempted to incorporate Jewish customs into the story. When Jeshua enters the home of Joseph's kin, Eleazar reminds him to touch the mezuzah. In accordance with the instructions of Deuteronomy 6:9 and 11:20, a scroll of scriptural passages (Deuteronomy 6:4–9 and often Deuteronomy 11:13–21) was traditionally enclosed in a case that was attached to the doorposts in a Jewish home. Customarily, the case is touched with the fingers, which are then kissed. Often a prayer is also offered with the touching of the mezuzah. The usual prayer, which Jeshua recites, is: "May God protect my going out and coming in, now and forever."[32]

As with modern Jews, ancient Jews very likely covered their heads during prayer. In the story I mentioned Eleazar's use of a tallit, or prayer shawl. In biblical times, the tallit, as such, did not exist. Individuals were commanded to sew fringes to the four corners of their outer garment (Deuteronomy 22:12). As clothing styles changed, the outer garment was replaced by the tallit. But since the actual name of such garments has been lost (and is never mentioned in the Bible), I took the liberty of calling Eleazar's garment a tallit, the name that eventually came to be used for the successor prayer shawls.

Luke records that Mary and Joseph were responding to the decree of the Roman emperor, Caesar Augustus, "that all the world should be taxed" (Luke 2:1–3). Rome required a census of its subjects. This served as the basis for the taxation of the empire's different peoples. Mary and Joseph could have registered at the city of their residence, Nazareth, but they adhered to the Jewish custom of returning to their ancestral home for the registration.[33]

Historically, there has been some disagreement over which census Luke refers to and when it actually occurred.[34] I personally believe that these problems derive more from the lack of adequate history than any error in Luke's account.[35]

Since both Mary and Joseph were of the royal Davidic line, they journeyed to the City of David, Bethlehem, in obedience to the decree. Mary was apparently close to delivery, "being great with child," when she and Joseph arrived (Luke 2:4–5). Because there was no room in the inn, the Lord was probably born in a stable (although the Bible never specifically mentions a stable). We do know that He was "laid in a manger," which certainly implies he was born in such a structure (Luke 2:7). It was here that the shepherds, heeding the instructions of the angel, found the child and His family (Luke 2:8–20). Tradition also holds that the stable was in a cave.

Unfortunately, the popular portrayals of the Nativity sometimes stray from the actual scriptural account, although admittedly the scriptures are often susceptible to different interpretations. For example, Christmas pageants almost universally depict the wise men visiting the stable after the shepherds. However, it is doubtful that Joseph would have allowed his family to live in such conditions for long. Since Bethlehem was the ancestral home of both Mary and Joseph, it seems probable that they would soon have located and stayed with some of their distant kin. Notwithstanding the depictions of the pageants, Matthew clearly states that the wise men came to a "house" where "they saw the young child" (Matthew 2:11).

The Greek word from which "house" is translated is *ŏikia* (οἰκία). That word is generally rendered as "residence," "abode," "home," "house," or "household."[36] In the story, I have taken that reference to a "house" literally, and the wise men visit the holy family in the home of Joseph's kin.

The Bible doesn't state how many Magi there were, but there are three gifts mentioned, and many traditions have long held that there were three wise men (although the number varies in some religions and traditions from two to twelve[37]). I elected to follow the general consensus of Western tradition and put three wise men in the story.

The account in Matthew begins with the Magi coming from the East, seeking Him who was "born King of the Jews" (Matthew 2:1–2). There is no mention of the child being the "Christ" until they arrive at Herod's court (Matthew 2:3–6). That set me to wondering if perhaps the wise men came seeking the King of the Jews only to find that the child was more than that—that He was, in fact, the long-awaited Messiah.

Through Herod's scribes and priests, accounts of angelic visitors, and their visit with the holy family, the wise men in the story come to a realization that the king they have been seeking is also the long-awaited Messiah. The actual Magi may have had some knowledge of Jewish writings and the Old Testament, and thus a familiarity with the prophecies of the Messiah. As a result of the first Diaspora, Jews were scattered among many of the countries from which the wise men are likely to have come. Indeed, although many believe the Magi to have been Zoroastrian priests, it may not be completely beyond the realm of possibility that they were

Jews, trained in the art of astrology. While the idea of Magi
with Jewish ties seems to have fallen out of vogue, early
commentators certainly posited such a possibility.[38]

The Bible is silent as to the names of the Magi. Western
tradition assigns them the names of Gaspar, Melchior, and
Balthasar (or variants thereof).[39] But the Syrian and Eastern traditions each attribute entirely different names to the
three. I chose to use the Syrian names, Hormisdas, Larvandad, and Gushnasaph,[40] simply because the names appear
to be Persian, and I personally think it likely that the Magi
came from the vicinity of Persia. Later writings also elevate
the wise men to the rank of kings, but they were more probably priests or scholars of the nobility.

There are likewise traditions regarding the symbolism
of the Magi's gifts. The Bible simply states that the gifts
were gold, frankincense, and myrrh, with no mention of any
symbolism. Perhaps the most popular tradition in this regard
maintains that gold was a symbol of Christ's kingship; frankincense, an incense, a symbol of His priesthood; and myrrh,
often used for embalming, a symbol of His death.[41] I do give a
nod to this tradition with the titles that the Magi express as
they bestow their gifts upon the Christ child. The wise man
who offers gold, states, "For the King of Kings" (referenc-
ing His kingship). The wise man who presents frankincense,
declares, "For the *Prince of Peace*" (an oblique reference to
His priesthood). *Prince of Peace* is, of course, one of the titles
Christ bore, but the title has sometimes been applied as well
to the ancient priest, Melchizedek, who was known as the
King of Salem or King of Peace. Christ would be "[c]alled of

God an *high priest* after the order of Melchisedec" (Hebrews 5:10; emphasis added). Finally, the third wise man, who gives the myrrh, states, "For the Redeemer of us all" (His death). Clearly, Christ's redemption came as a result of Him offering His life on the cross. The Atonement was only made possible through His death.

Matthew states that the wise men had "seen his star in the east" (Matthew 2:2), and that the star apparently reappeared after their departure from Jerusalem and went before them, till it came and stood over where the young child was" (Matthew 2:9). There are numerous theories as to what the star was and when it appeared. Many hold that the star was merely a conjunction of planets, a comet, or some similar manifestation.[42] I think the biblical account is more consistent with an apparently unrecorded "new" star, perhaps a nova, supernova, or some other cataclysmic stellar event. And, for the purposes of the narrative, such a star is much more dramatic than something like a conjunction. So in the story, I describe a "new" star, but am purposely vague as to its characteristics. I use a clearing of overcast skies to account for the star's apparent reappearance after the coming of the Magi, but I might also have relied on the fact that such stars can sometimes fluctuate in magnitude.

The length of the time interval between Christ's birth and the wise men's arrival is an interesting question. The biblical account would lead us to believe that a fair amount of time elapsed. The wise men were "from the east" and apparently had some distance to travel after seeing "his star" (Matthew 2:1–2). Various Christian churches have different traditions and beliefs regarding the time of the advent of the Magi. Many believe the Magi visited mere days after Jesus' birth. Their coming is often celebrated at the time of the Feast of the Epiphany, usually twelve days after Christmas. Others believe the Magi took over a year to arrive.[43]

Luke describes a number of events that occurred after the birth of Jesus, including His circumcision at eight days, when He was officially named, and His presentation at the temple in Jerusalem, after the days of Mary's purification under "the law of Moses were accomplished" (Luke 2:21–22). Jewish law required that the firstborn son be ransomed with a sacrifice at the temple (Luke 2:23–24), if possible. This was done, in the case of Jesus, at the temple in Jerusalem, with the offering of two turtledoves or pigeons. In connection with this visit to Jerusalem, Luke also recounts the prophetic utterances of Simeon and Anna (Luke 2:25–38). The days of purification, according to Leviticus, took some forty days (Leviticus 12:1–4). Since the presentation in the temple was not made until the days of Mary's purification were accomplished, this means that Christ's presentation occurred at least forty days after His birth.

That all of these events transpired before the coming of the wise men seems evident from Matthew's account that Joseph, as soon as the wise men "were departed," was warned by an angel in a dream to take Mary and the child and "flee into Egypt" to escape the wrath of Herod (Matthew 2:12–15). It is doubtful that the wicked Herod would have delayed very long his slaughter of the innocents, and equally doubtful that Jesus' parents would have risked His life by tarrying to present Jesus at the temple. In fact, Matthew's narrative seems to suggest that Joseph arose from his dream and departed for Egypt that very night (Matthew 2:13–14).

Also, the sacrifice at the temple was the one permitted for those who were impoverished—two turtledoves or pigeons—rather than the more expensive lamb and a turtledove or pigeon (Leviticus 12:6–8).[44] Had the Magi come before the presentation at the temple, the family would have had the resources for the more costly sacrifice. So if, as it appears, Jesus' presentation at the temple indeed preceded the Magi's coming, this would mean they did not come until at least forty days after Jesus' birth.

When the wise men first arrived in Judaea, seeking Him who was "born King of the Jews," they innocently sought the newborn king in Jerusalem (Matthew 2:1–2). Herod the Great was evidently "troubled" when he heard of the mission of the Magi (Matthew 2:3). Under the protection of Rome, Herod, an Idumaean, had become king of much of Palestine, including Judaea, Galilee, Samaria, Idumaea, and Peraea. He was not a ruler who would suffer any challenge to his throne. He had, after all, already put to death two of his own sons, whom he perceived had aspirations to his throne, and would soon have his oldest son killed.[45]

Herod "privily" summoned the wise men to inquire as to the particulars of the star's appearance. Matthew's two references to Jerusalem (Matthew 2:1, 3) in the account of the Magi make it clear that this meeting occurred at Herod's palace in Jerusalem and not at his summer palace, several miles southeast of Bethlehem. After Herod had obtained what information he could from the wise men, he then directed them to Bethlehem as the prophesied birthplace of the Messiah. He, of course, also asked that when they had "found him, bring me word again, that I may come and worship him also" (Matthew 2:7–8). Herod certainly wanted to know the location of the child, although worshiping Him was undoubtedly not his primary objective.

That Herod "slew all the children that were in Bethlehem, and in all the coasts thereof, from two years old and under, according to the time which he had diligently enquired of the wise men" (Matthew 2:16), indicates it may have taken the Magi as long as two years after Jesus' birth to arrive. However, it is easy to imagine that the crafty and heartless Herod gave himself a margin of error in selecting the age of the children to kill. In the story, I don't precisely indicate how long after the birth of Jesus the wise men appear, but I intimate a period of greater than six weeks, which seems reasonable.

Finally, there is the issue of what time of year the birth of Jesus occurred. It is unlikely that it occurred on December 25. That day was apparently chosen to replace a Roman pagan holiday.[46] Interestingly, a number of the earliest Christian writers assign the date of the birth to March, April, or May.[47] While it appears certain that the decree of Augustus would have taken a lengthy period of time to implement, it also seems doubtful that the authorities would have begun the census in the dead of winter. In the story, I indicate that Jesus' birth occurred in the spring. The fact that the shepherds were "in the field, keeping watch over their flock by night" (Luke 2:8) does make a spring birth seem plausible.

End Notes

1. Randall J. Buth, "Aramaic Language," *Dictionary of New Testament Background*, ed. Craig A. Evans and Stanley E. Porter (Downers Grove, IL: InterVarsity Press, 2000), 87–89; Edward P. Sanders and Jaroslav Jan Pelikan, "Jesus: The Christ and Christology," *The New Encyclopædia Britannica*, 15th ed., 32 vols. (Chicago: Encyclopedia Britannica, Inc., 2005), 22:337.

2. Frederick E. Greenspahn, *An Introduction to Aramaic*, 2nd ed. (Atlanta: Society of Biblical Literature, 2003), 5–7.

3. *Webster's Third New International Dictionary of the English Language*, Unabridged (Springfield, MA· Merriam-Webster Inc., 2002), s.v. "Aramaic," definition 2.

4. Buth, "Aramaic Language," *Dictionary of New Testament Background*, 89–90; J. R. Porter, *Jesus Christ: The Jesus of History, the Christ of Faith* (New York: Oxford University Press, 1999), 46–47.

5. Paul L. Redditt, "Jeshua," *Eerdmans Dictionary of the Bible*, ed. David Noel Freedman, Allen C. Myers, and Astrid B. Beck (Grand Rapids: William B. Eerdmans Publishing Co., 2000) 700–701; John M. Court and

Kathleen M. Court, "Jesus," *The Penguin Dictionary of the Bible* (London: Penguin Group, 2007) 168; *The Oxford English Dictionary*, 2nd ed. 20 vols. (Oxford: Oxford University Press, 1989), s.v. "Jesus."

6. J. D. Douglas et al., ed., "Jeshua, Jeshuah," *The New International Dictionary of the Bible: Pictorial Edition* (Grand Rapids: Regency Reference Library, 1987), 523–24.

7. *Oxford English Dictionary*, s.v. "Jesus."

8. J. R. Porter, *Jesus Christ*, 47.

9. *The Random House Dictionary of the English Language* (New York: Random House, Inc., 1967), s.v. "Jesus."

10. *The Oxford Bible Reader's Dictionary & Concordance* (Oxford: Oxford University Press), s.vv. "Jeshua," "Jesus."

11. John L. McKenzie, "Jesus Christ," *Dictionary of the Bible* (Milwaukee: The Bruce Publishing Company, 1965), 432; William Smith, "Jeshua," "Jesus," and "Jesus Christ," *A Dictionary of the Bible*, ed. F. N. Peloubet and M. A. Peloubet (Nashville: Thomas Nelson Publishers, 1979), 306–307.

12. Everett F. Harrison, "Christ, Jesus," *The New International Dictionary of the Bible*, 203.

13. *Oxford English Dictionary*, s.v. "Jesus."

14. James Strong, "Hebrew and Chaldee Dictionary of the Old Testament," *Strong's New Exhaustive Concordance of the Bible* (Iowa Falls, IA: World Bible Publishers, Inc., 1986), s.v. entry 3091, "Yehowshuwa or Yehowshua."

15. *Oxford English Dictionary*, s.v. "Jesus."

16. Smith, "Jesus," cf. "Joshua," *A Dictionary of the Bible*, 307 and 323.

17. *The Random House Dictionary of the English Language*, s.v. "Jesus."

18. Gerhard Kittel, ed., *Theological Dictionary of the New Testament*, trans. and ed. Geoffrey W. Bromiley (Grand Rapids: Wm. B. Eerdmans Publishing Company, 1965), s.v. "Ἰησοῦς." 284.

19. Strong, "Greek Dictionary of the New Testament," *Strong's New Exhaustive Concordance*, s.v. entry 5547, "Χριστός Christŏs."

20. Frederick W. Norris, "Christ, Christology," *Encyclopedia of Early Christianity*, 2nd ed., 2 vols., ed. Everett Ferguson, Michael P. McHugh, and Frederick W. Norris (New York and London: Garland Publishing, Inc., 1997), 1:242.

21. E. P. Sanders, "Jesus Christ," *Eerdmans Dictionary of the Bible*, 701.

22. Sanders and Pelikan, "Jesus: The Christ and Christology," *The New Encyclopædia Britannica*, 22:336; Norris, "Christ, Christology," *Encyclopedia of Early Christianity*, 1:242.

23. McKenzie, "Jesus Christ," *Dictionary of the Bible*, 432.

24. Ronald Brownrigg, "Barnabas," in "Who's Who in the New Testament," Joan Comay and Ronald Brownrigg, *Who's Who in the Bible*, 2 vols. in one (New York: Wings Books, 1993), 2:69.

25. J. R. Porter, *Jesus Christ*, 46–47.

26. Viacom International, Inc., "Aramaic Names," ParentsConnect, s.vv. "Shapira," "Tabitha," "Toma," http://babynamesworld.parentsconnect.com/aramaic-names–5.html (accessed March 22, 2010).

27. *Aramaic Lexicon and Concordance*, Atour: The State of Assyria, s.v. "Mary" "Myrm," word number 12456, http://www.atour.com/cgi-bin/lexicon.cgi (accessed October 6, 2008).

28. *Oxford English Dictionary*, s.v. "Mary."

29. F. F. Bruce, "Genealogy of Jesus Christ," *New Bible*

Dictionary, 3rd ed., ed. D. R. W. Wood et al. (Leicester, Eng.: Inter-Varsity Press, 1996), 402.

30. James E. Talmage, *Jesus the Christ*, 38th ed. (Winchester, Mass.: University Press, 1971), 89–90 n. 5.

31. Talmage, *Jesus the Christ*, 89–90 n. 5; Bruce, "Genealogy of Jesus Christ," *New Bible Dictionary*, 402.

32. Harvey Lutske, *The Book of Jewish Customs* (Northvale, NJ: Jason Aronson Inc., 1986), 179.

33. Talmage, *Jesus the Christ*, 91–92.

34. Stanley E. Porter, "Chronology, New Testament," *Dictionary of New Testament Background*, 201–202.

35. Ibid., see page 202 for a very interesting discussion on this point.

36. Strong, "Main Concordance," *Strong's New Exhaustive Concordance of the Bible*, s.v. "House," entry for Matthew 2:11; Strong, "Greek Dictionary of the New Testament," *Strong's New Exhaustive Concordance of the Bible*, s.v. entry 3614, "οἰκία."

37. Jacques Duchense-Guillemin, Edward John Joyce, and Margaret Stevenson, "Magi," *The New Catholic Encyclopedia*, 2nd ed., 15 vols., ed. Thomas Carson, et al. (Farmington Hills, MI.: Gale, 2003), 9:34.

38. Adam Clarke, *(Clarke's Commentary) The New Testament of Our Lord and Saviour Jesus Christ: The Text Carefully Printed from the Most Correct Copies of the Present Authorized Translation, Including the Marginal Readings and Parallel Texts; with a Commentary and Critical Notes; Designed as a Help to a Better Understanding of the Sacred Writings*, 6 vols. (Nashville: Abingdon, n.d.) 5:43.

39. Walter Drum, "Magi," *The Catholic Encyclopedia*, 15 vols., ed. Charles G. Herbermann et al. (New York: Robert Appleton Company, 1910), 9:528.

40. Drum, "Magi," *The Catholic Encyclopedia*, 9:528.

41. Talmage, *Jesus the Christ*, 108 n. 4; Talmage is quick to assert that there is no scriptural basis for ascribing any symbolism to the gifts. Yet many continue to see such symbolism. For some, frankincense is a symbol of deity, rather than priesthood. For example, in the beloved American carol "We Three Kings of Orient Are," written in 1857 by the Reverend John Henry Hopkins, gold is for Christ's royalty, frankincense "owns a Deity nigh," and myrrh is for the Lord's death

42. M. T. Fermer, "Stars," *New Bible Dictionary*, 1132.

43. Drum, "Magi," *The Catholic Encyclopedia*, 9:528–29.

44. Talmage, *Jesus the Christ*, 96; Howard F. Vos, *Nelson's New Illustrated Bible Manners & Customs* (Nashville: Thomas Nelson, Inc., 1999), 451.

45. Adrian Leske, "Matthew," *The International Bible Commentary: A Catholic and Ecumenical Commentary for the Twenty-First Century*, ed. William R. Farmer et al. (Collegeville, MN: The Liturgical Press, 1998), 1262.

46. Richard Lonergan Foley, "Nativity of Christ," *The New Catholic Encyclopedia*, 10:173.

47. Susan K. Roll, "Christmas and Its Cycle," *The New Catholic Encyclopedia*, 3:551; Hendrik F. Stander, "Christmas," *Encyclopedia of Early Christianity*, 1:251.

$\mathscr{A}$cknowledgments

I originally conceived the idea for this story some twenty-five years ago as my family and I drove home after spending Christmas with my sister, Pam, and her family. That evening, I wrote the ending on a piece of paper, which I promptly lost. Fifteen years later, while working evenings and weekends at a children's urgent care, I began committing the story to paper as a way to wind down after coming home late at night. I fortunately was able to recreate the ending. After I finished the story, that next Christmas I gave everyone a copy and thought that would be the last anyone would ever see of Jeshua Barnabas and his Christmas adventure.

Over the last several years, I have been working on a biography, *Cyclone*—the story of my father, Col. Emmett S. "Cyclone" Davis, a famous World War II fighter pilot. A couple of years ago, as Christmas approached, several members of my family encouraged me to resurrect *The Fourth Gift*. As I read over the original version, I decided the story could be expanded and might be publishable. So, I interrupted my work on *Cyclone* and set about further developing the story and characters, while attempting to capture the flavor of first-century Bethlehem. The result was this little Christmas story in its current form.

I must first thank my niece Summer Mull, who alerted me to the fact that Cedar Fort was looking for Christmas projects. Next, I must thank Liz Carlston, a long-time friend of Summer and our family, for pitching *The Fourth Gift* to Cedar Fort and for continuing to promote the work. And finally I would like to thank the wonderful folks at Cedar Fort and Bonneville Books for enthusiastically embracing this book and moving it to publication. In particular, I should thank Lyle Mortimer, Jennifer Fielding, Heather Holm, Sheralyn Pratt, Megan Whittier for her striking and elegant cover design, and especially my editor, Heidi Doxey, who not only did the beautiful typesetting but patiently coaxed me through the final polishing of the manuscript.

Not long after I had written the first version of *The Fourth Gift*, I saw Joseph Brickey's exquisite painting, "Silent Night." I immediately exclaimed, "That's my beggar boy!" I knew his depiction of that holy night had to be my cover illustration and I am very grateful that the talent of Mr. Brickey now graces the front of this book.

I am indebted to my sister, Pamela Mull, "a highly paid professional" as she likes to remind me, for her many hours spent reviewing my feeble attempts at revision. Likewise, I am grateful for the encouragement and efforts of a noted author, my nephew Brandon Mull, who was an early champion of this work. I am also appreciative of dear friends Bob and Karen Terashima and their staff for enabling me to write while I practice medicine.

I must also thank my niece Tiffany Mull, one of my original readers, who carefully preserved a copy of the first manuscript, and my nephew Ty Mull, who offered insightful editorial advice.

Early readers of the work who provided invaluable suggestions and encouragement include: Cy and Marge Davis, Kimberlee Richards, Jeannie Williams, Gary Mull, Mary Mull, Bryson and Cherie Mull, Gladys Mull, Trudy Walton, and Pam Aupiu.

I sincerely hope this story brightens your Christmas and helps recall those momentous events of two thousand years ago. May we all learn to sacrifice a little more in behalf of those we love.

Finally, I would be remiss not to offer my profound thanks for a Father who gave us His Only Begotten Son, and for that Son, who would give His life to redeem us all.